Supporting Learning in Schools

D1464145

Hampshire
County Council

Rising Stars UK Ltd.
22 Grafton Street, London W1S 4EX
www.risingstars-uk.com

The right of Roger Hurn to be identified as the author of this work
has been asserted by him in accordance with the Copyright, Design
and Patents Act 1988.

Published 2007

Cover design: Button plc
Illustrator: Stik, Bill Greenhead for Illustration
Text design and typesetting: Andy Wilson
Publisher: Gill Budgell
Publishing manager: Sasha Morton
Editor: Catherine Baker
Series consultant: Cliff Moon

British Library Cataloguing in Publication Data.
A CIP record for this book is available from the British Library

ISBN: 978-1-84680-228-7

Printed in the UK by CPI Bookmarque, Croydon, CR0 4TD

Mixed Sources
Product group from well-managed
forests and other controlled sources
www.fsc.org Cert no. TT-COC-002227
© 1996 Forest Stewardship Council
FSC

Contents

Meet the Mystery Mob

Name:

Gummy

FYI: Gummy hasn't got much brain – and even fewer teeth.

Loves: Soup.

Hates: Toffee chews.

Fact: The brightest thing about him is his shirt.

Name:

Lee

FYI: If Lee was any cooler he'd be a cucumber.

Loves: Hip-hop.

Hates: Hopscotch.

Fact: He has his own designer label (which he peeled off a tin).

Name:

FYI: Rob lives in his own world – he's just visiting planet Earth.

Loves: Daydreaming.

Hates: Nightmares.

Fact: Rob always does his homework – he just forgets to write it down.

Name:

FYI: Dwayne is smarter than a tree full of owls.

Loves: Anything complicated.

Hates: Join-the-dots books.

Fact: If he was any brighter you could use him as a floodlight at football matches.

Name:

Chet

FYI: Chet is as brave as a lion with steel jaws.

Loves: Having adventures.

Hates: Knitting.

Fact: He's as tough as the chicken his granny cooks for his tea.

Name:

Adi

FYI: Adi is as happy as a football fan with tickets to the big match.

Loves: Telling jokes.

Hates: Moaning minnies.

Fact: He knows more jokes than a jumbo joke book.

The Big Parade

The circus has come to town.
The Mystery Mob are watching
the big parade. All the acts are wearing
colourful costumes. There are fire-eaters,
clowns, jugglers, acrobats, stilt-walkers
and a very loud band. The boys think
it's totally awesome!

Adi   Hey, do you know why
           clowns wear loud socks?

Rob   I haven't got a clue.

Adi   So their feet don't go to sleep!

Mystery Mob
           Duh!

Lee You should work in the circus, Adi.

Adi Too right! I'm funnier than any of the clowns.

Lee No, I meant as a human cannonball. Then we could fire you for making awful jokes.

Adi Yeah, yeah – whatever. But I still can't wait to see the show tonight.

Rob Me too.

Gummy I want to see the sword swallower. I reckon I could do that.

Dwayne Only because you've got no front teeth.

Adi Only because he's got no brain, you mean.

Gummy Are you saying I'm daft?

Adi No, just a few fries short of a happy meal, that's all.

Gummy That reminds me – I'm hungry. Who's coming for a burger?

Rob, Lee and Dwayne go off
with Gummy, but Chet and Adi
want to follow the circus parade.

Chet   Let's go and see the Big Top.

Adi   What's a Big Top?

Chet   It's the tent where the circus guys
put on their show. We can sneak
inside and see them trying out
their acts.

Adi   Great idea. Hey, what's this?

Adi points at a Wanted poster on a wall.

Chet   It's a Wanted poster
for Robin Desafe,
the famous bank robber.

Adi   Yeah, he's escaped from jail
and gone on the run.
The cops are looking everywhere
for him. I saw it on the news
this morning.

Chet Wow, he looks mean.
I wonder where he's hiding out?
I wouldn't want to bump into him
down a dark alley.

Adi There's no chance of that
happening. We're going
to the circus – not down
a dark alley. But the others
will be hopping mad
when they find out we've seen
the show for free.

Chet Even if it is only
the dress rehearsal.

Adi   Yes. Hey, did you hear
about the boy who ran off
with the circus?

Chet   No – what happened?

Adi   The police made him give it back!

Chet   I wish you'd run off
with the circus.

Adi   Well, I'm going to run
after the circus.
Catch me if you can!

❷

The Big Top

Chet and Adi are outside the Big Top.
They can hear loud music coming
from inside the tent.

Chet   I'm really glad circuses
don't have performing animals
any more.

Adi   Why's that?

Chet   Because I think it's cruel
to make animals perform tricks.
Lions and tigers and elephants
belong in the jungle,
not in a circus.

Adi You're right. But it isn't cruel to let animals watch humans doing tricks, is it?

Chet I don't think so.

Adi That's good, because I've got my pet mouse Jumbo in my pocket. I'm going to let him see the show. I think he'll love it.

Chet Sometimes I really worry about you, Adi.

Adi   No. You need to worry about important stuff – like how are we going to get inside the Big Top without a ticket?

Chet   That's easy. We can lift up this bit of the tent and crawl inside while nobody's looking.

Adi   But what if someone does see us?

Chet   No problem. We'll say we're
trying to catch your pet mouse.
It's just escaped from your pocket
and run into the tent.

Adi   But Jumbo hasn't escaped.
Look, here he is.

Adi puts his hand into his pocket.
He pulls out a small, white mouse.
It has long whiskers and a pink nose.

The mouse sits up. It sniffs the air,
and then jumps out of Adi's hands.
It lands on the grass and races off
into the Big Top.

Chet   I don't believe it!

Adi   Don't just stand there, Chet.
We've got to get him back.
Jumbo's never been out
on his own before. He'll get lost!

The boys dive under the tent flap
after Jumbo.

Who Threw
all the Pies?

The boys peep out from behind
a row of empty seats. In the circus ring,
Biffo the clown is standing next to
a table piled high with custard pies.
Adi spots Jumbo. He's sitting on
Biffo's hat. The trouble is –
Biffo is wearing the hat!

Adi	We need to find a way to grab Jumbo off Biffo's hat without Biffo seeing us.
Chet	How are we going to do that?
Adi	That's easy. We'll slip into the ring, tiptoe up to the table, grab two of those custard pies and throw them at Biffo. Then, while he's wiping custard from his face, we'll nab Jumbo. We'll be out of there before Biffo knows what's hit him.
Chet	Good plan. Let's do it!

Adi and Chet pick up the pies
and hurl them at Biffo. Splat! Adi's pie
is a direct hit. The plan is working.
Biffo's face is covered in gloopy custard.
He can't see a thing. But Chet's pie
knocks Biffo's hat off. Jumbo falls through
the air. He lands with a splash in the pie.

Adi   You twit. Now I've got
a custard- flavoured mouse.

Chet   Don't worry. Jumbo's safe.
Cats can't stand the taste
of custard.

Adi   Very funny. But there's no time
to lose. We've got to get Jumbo
out of that pie. I don't think
he can swim.

Chet and Adi dash into the ring
but don't see the big banana skin
that is lying on the floor. It has fallen out
of Biffo's pocket. They both step on it.

Chet and Adi

AAAARRRRGGGHHHH!!!!!!!

Crash! The boys skid into the table.
The custard pies fly up in the air.
Splosh! They land on Chet and Adi.
Both boys are smothered in yucky
yellow goo. Chet and Adi have
soggy custard in their hair, their eyes,
their ears and up their noses!

But that's not all. Biffo is standing
over them. When he wiped the custard
off his face he also wiped off his
clown make-up by mistake. The boys can
now see his real face –
and he isn't laughing!

It's a Knockout

Adi   You're not Biffo – you're
Robin Desafe!

Robin   Grrr ... you've seen through
my perfect disguise.

Chet   What have you done with
the real Biffo, you crook?

Robin   He's locked in his caravan.
I've tied him up and taken his
place. The police are looking
for a bank robber – not a clown.

Adi   So what are you going to do
with us?

Robin   Welcome to the Circus of Doom,
boys. You sneaked in without
tickets so nobody knows you're
here. I'm going to lock you up
with Biffo. His jokes are so
unfunny he'll bore you to death!

Chet grabs a large bucket that
is on the ground next to him.

Chet   Don't move or I'll chuck this bucket of water all over you.

Robin   Go ahead – that bucket's empty.

Chet   Oh no it's not.

Robin   Oh yes it is.

Adi   Hey, this is a circus – not a pantomime.

Robin   What are you on about, you idiot?

While he stops to glare at Adi,
Chet rams the bucket on to Robin's head.

Robin   Urgh!

Chet   I told you it wasn't empty.
            It's full of a crook's head.

Robin staggers around the circus ring
trying to pull the bucket off. Then he trips
and falls over. The bucket makes
a really loud clang as Robin's head
hits the ground.

Adi   Ouch. That must have hurt.
I can see stars going round
the bucket!

Chet   Yep. He's knocked himself out
cold. He's not going anywhere
for a bit, so come on.
Let's free the real Biffo
and send for the cops
before Robin wakes up!

But then Adi spots Jumbo.
The little mouse is running up a rope
that leads to the high wire!

Adi   Sorry, Chet. No can do.
           Jumbo's up on the high wire.
           He'll fall if I don't save him.

Before Chet can stop him, Adi starts
to climb up the ladder to the tightrope.
But if Adi falls off the tightrope
this really will be a circus of doom –
for him!

5

The Highwire

When Adi gets up to the top of the ladder,
he sees Jumbo sitting on the wire
just out of his reach. There's only
one thing for it. To save his pet mouse,
Adi must walk the tightrope.
He looks down and sees Chet looking
up at him. It's a long way
back down to the ground.
Adi gulps.

Chet Take care, Adi. Try not to fall off.

Adi That's a brilliant idea, Chet.
Why didn't I think of that?

Chet Stretch your arms out.
That'll help you keep
your balance.

Adi Okay. Here I go.

Adi steps on to the tightrope. It wobbles.
Adi wobbles. Jumbo wobbles. Jumbo grips
the rope with his claws. Adi hasn't
got any claws to grip with. He waves his
arms in the air. This doesn't help.
It makes him wobble even more.
Then he falls off.

Adi   (shouting) *HELP!*

But just in time Adi grabs at the rope.
He stops falling and dangles in the air.

Chet Don't let go of the rope, Adi.

Adi That's another top idea.
I don't know how you keep
thinking them up. So I'm going
to just hang around here while
you figure out how you're going
to get me out of this mess – and
save Jumbo.

But Jumbo is fed up with tightrope walking. He scuttles along the rope and runs down Adi's arm and back into Adi's pocket. He's safe – but Adi isn't.

Adi Oh no. All that custard is making my hands slippery. I can't hold on any longer!

Chet You've got to. It's way too far to fall!

Chet is too busy looking up at Adi
to notice that Robin has woken up.
Robin pulls the bucket off his head.
He is really angry. He creeps up
behind Chet. Robin has an evil look
on his ugly face.

Adi   It's no good, Chet. I'm done for!
              Arghhhhhhh!

Chet   Noooooooooo!

Adi tumbles down. He lands smack on top of Robin. Robin is flattened!

Adi　Hey, I think a bank robber just saved my life.

Chet　Yeah, but I don't think he meant to. You've KO'ed him. And that serves him right. When he wakes up he'll be back in jail.

Adi Hmmm … but I think this is one bank robber who'll be glad to be back in prison.

Chet What makes you say that?

Adi Well, let's face it, this circus has been nothing but a great big headache for him!

About the author

Roger Hurn has:

- been an actor in 'The Exploding Trouser Company'
- played bass guitar in a rock band
- been given the title Malam Oga (wise teacher, big boss!) while on a storytelling trip to Africa.

Now he's a writer, and he hopes you like reading about the Mystery Mob as much as he likes writing about them.

The Big Top
circus quiz

Questions

1 Who is in charge of a circus?

2 What is the Big Top?

3 Where do circus artists perform their acts?

4 Can you name three or more things that clowns wear?

5 What do we call the person who walks on the high wire?

6 What do we call the swing acrobats use in their act?

7 Why wouldn't you want a ride in a clown's car?

8 In the song which famous elephant packed her trunk and said goodbye to the circus?

Answers

1 The Ringmaster.
2 The main tent of a circus.
3 In the circus ring.
4 Big boots, red noses, silly wigs, brightly-coloured trousers, braces, daft hats, flowers that squirt water.
5 A tightrope walker.
6 A flying trapeze.
7 It always breaks down.
8 Nellie the Elephant.

How did you score?

✋ If you got all eight answers correct, then you could be the Ringmaster in a circus!

✋ If you got six answers correct, you could be a circus performer.

✋ If you got fewer than four answers correct, you've been spending too much time hanging out with the clowns!

41

When I was a kid

Question Did you ever go to the circus
when you were a kid?

Roger No.

Question Why not?

Roger I couldn't find it.

Question Why didn't you ask someone?

Roger I did. I said, "How do I get to
the circus?"

Question What did they say?

Roger They said I had to practise very hard.

Question Well, have you ever seen clowns?

Roger Yes. I once saw two of them
walk into the Big Top.
I was surprised.

Question Why?

Roger I thought they should have seen it.

Adi's favourite circus joke

Why don't you ever see elephants at the circus?

Because they much prefer going to the movies!

How to be a circus star

 If you want to be a fire-eater always keep a bucket of water handy.

 Avoid butter if you want to be a juggler.

 Always wear a parachute if you want to be a trapeze artist.

If you want to be a clown:

 Buy a big red nose (or catch
a terrible cold).

 Buy shoes ten sizes too big for you.

 Make sure your trousers don't fit.

 Wear polka-dot underpants.

 Buy a car with square wheels
and a steering wheel that keeps coming off
– but don't join the AA.

Fantastic facts about the circus

1 An Englishman called Philip Astley invented the first circus in 1772. His circus had horses, rope dancers, clowns, jugglers and acrobats.

2 Horses were the stars of the first circuses. They danced to music.

3 Circuses became more dangerous when wild animals like lions, tigers and elephants became part of the show.

4 In 2006 a law was passed to stop wild animals doing tricks in circuses.

5 Clowns with white face make-up always get the better of the other clowns. They're the smart ones – which isn't saying much.

Circus lingo

Big Top This is the tent where the circus acts perform. It is not an extra-large T-shirt.

Main guy This is the rope that holds up the centre pole in the Big Top. The main guy is not the man in charge – that's the Ringmaster.

Ringmaster This is the man in charge of the show. He is nothing to do with hobbits or Middle Earth.

Roustabout This is someone who works doing odd jobs for the circus. A Roustabout is not a traffic island.

Sledge gang This is the crew of men who hammer in the tent stakes. They are not bank robbers who drive a getaway toboggan.

Troupers These are the circus entertainers. If you like their acts they are Super Troupers. If not, they are Pooper Troupers.

Mystery Mob

   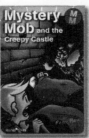

  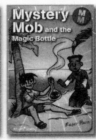 

RISING ★ STARS